Sweating It Out

poems by

Deborah Turner

Finishing Line Press
Georgetown, Kentucky

Sweating It Out

ACKNOWLEDGMENTS

One poem, "When I Arise Glistening," first appeared in Patrice Vecchione's *The Body Eclectic: An Anthology of Poems* (Henry Holt and Company LTD). The author thanks her and others who made its inclusion in that volume possible. The author also thanks those responsible for the gospel song quoted within it. She sang it in a childhood choir, yet has been unable to identify its source.

Publisher: Leah Maines
Editor: Christen Kincaid
Cover Art: Harrison Haines from Pexels
Author Photo: Stephanie Stefanik
Cover Design: Elizabeth Maines McCleavy

Order online: www.finishinglinepress.com
also available on amazon.com

Author inquiries and mail orders:
Finishing Line Press
P. O. Box 1626
Georgetown, Kentucky 40324
U. S. A.

Table of Contents

Juneteenth.. 1

Double Dutch... 2

My Son's Avatar.. 4

Something from Nothin 5

Black Patriarch... 7

Consumption 8

Time Out 10

From the Lighthouse... 13

Coming Down 14

Sidelined 15

Switch Hitting 16

When I Arise.. 17

Juneteenth

Some come for the music.
Some for the somethin
      from nothin recipes,
two, three centuries old,
nourishment like a hug
from the ancestors.

Some come to make money
Some to spend…
      "made this one maself,
        half price today,"
twinkle in her deep brown
spies the bill stamped "Black money."
This time, they really do reap
what they sow.

Some come for the crowds.
Some for green, open space,
      warm, inviting talk
      and a chance
      to see all in the absence of urgency.
And the children run free
like schools of sardines
lacing the kelp-like crowd in jubilee.
And the ancestors, smiling,
whisper in trees, say
sun rays
ease my pain
let me rest in peace.

Double Dutch

LaTasha
lives her life
like a game
of double dutch.
She watches
its rhythm
for the time
to jump in.

And she knows
when to jump in.

                Hey!

Got two girlfriends
turning rope
as she hops nimble,

                Yeah!

not letting twirling twine
come between
her pulsing connection
with the earth.

                Well…

World outside them ropes
ain't even there.

                No, it ain't!

And her—
braids bouncin
legs twitchin,
so steady, so stealth,
you'd think she was standing still,

                Sho nuff did.

like he does
at night.

                              Say what?

LaTasha knows
he don't know
how to use
his wooden handle.

                              No he don't.

So she pretends
It's her turn to twirl
and the game ends
with rain.

But really,

                              Tell it, Honey.

she's watching
the rhythm
cause she knows
when it's time
to jump in.

                              Go Girl.
                              You, go girl.

My Son's Avatar

I was surprised to see a pale hour-glass of a girl
in our living room.
Her red pigtail bobbed as she attacked the wall with an ax.
After her, a burly black boy's dreadlocks also bounced
as he knocked down the door to the kitchen.
Still later, a freckle-faced tattooed white kid, then
a svelte black girl advanced through the rubble to fell the garage.
In shambles, the remains on the screen
resembled my son's room.
As axes changed to M16s, I took solace
at what superior focus my son had
before he got killed
and at how, at least, he wasn't asking for money.
And I try to recall what a decade of burning bras
and another of fighting, to make our lives matter,
meant. Were we seeking this kind of choice?
Is this what we meant when we wished
they could stand in our shoes?

Something from Nothin
for David Lawrence

Long after the draft and regular paychecks
put an end to punching two time clocks,
long before many daughters and, at last, a son,
he traded second shift for hobby,
corner store broom for rec court racket,
acquired ivory accessories like bourgeois badges,
watched Arthur Ashe like it coulda been him
then later, silver spoon fed it all to his oldest
until she choked and traded bonding for boys.

Long after her own paychecks flowed,
she came into a racket
too easily to understand longing.
Knowing little of sweeping
  and less of the game,
she played as if
it weren't a reunion.
In time, she found her way
to front court and backhands,
to white skorts and
the quiet of each set.

Eventually, the two squared off—
her gaining skills, him losing somethin.
They matched ace for ace,
traded line drives for lobs,
until their bodies began to glisten.
Finally, a cautious serve,
slow and inviting,
a volley ensued
smooth as a grandfather clock tocking.
It went on like that
until, hypnotized,
both desired to win.
So they kept
It always turned out the same—

Love, love,
which they mistook
for nothing.

Black Patriarch

She used to think him
snake-like, shedding
families like skin,

but came to see
he parents like a cloud.
Watch it shrink back,
while expanding, and grow
into afternoon rain that
tickles, so soft eyes don't see it
dissipate, form anew
over another
so in need
of water and shade.

Consumption

Show me
one of those
cute little
USA Today diagrams
dissecting
a broken promise.

Show me
a blotted bar graph
boxing scenes
in a dream deferred.

Print me some proof
that purchasing power
means more than
a wish, a prayer
and a lottery ticket.

Tell me
where to draw
the line, graph
distance between
credit and welfare.

Feed me a slice
of that
3-days-til-pay-day
air pudding pie chart.

Oh and please
use some
powerful reds, vivacious violets,
bathe me in yellows,
soothe me in deep browns
and green.

Cause I'm sick and tired of
        "I can't afford it"
        "Maybe when I get a raise"
        "Come payday we'll be alright"
I'm sick and tired of those consuming blues.

So just, please, show me
        one of those
        neat, succinct
        USA Today diagrams
        dissecting a dream deferred.

Time Out

The endless anticipating comes to a stop first
followed, reluctantly, by the double checking,
the enduring deferring,
the sad second guessing and tirelessly looking over your shoulder,
which you suddenly realize you've done your whole life,
can't recall when you didn't,
as you try to stick to an extended exhale.

A single thought breaks
the quiet attention
what if...
...a straight strand of hair coils
...skin dries up to ashy
...a pleasing look grows placid—
When your meditation teacher sees, prompts
you to soften your eyelids, you wonder
if she notices your legs aren't all that's cross.

With further prompting, you hold
what little you've gained
by overdoing—overdressing, over smiling,
    over ingratiating—
and you contemplate
how it helped you avoid under whelming
    and miss being dismissed.

Again you try
to exhale the discomfort of being the only one,
to let go of glances you've gotten for not playing,
not sharing what you know
with the bosses around you—
    for, though younger and unknown,
    they surely will advance farther, faster
    regardless of where—

and you try to release
how you learned to disappear, politely open
doors or stand close
to cleaning carts until colleagues assume
you're not one of them
despite having just left the same meeting
in which only the lookalikes
got a word in edgewise.

And slowly,
one by one, lessons of assimilating
fly up and out the mediation retreat window,
taking with them the good sense your mama made you
promise to use,
until you've lifted off the cushioned zafu—
ever too small for your God-given Black behind.
Mindfully being human
is not what you expected.
Sitting in stillness
you practice
not playing nice.

With a deep inhale, you hold the question
how am I to enjoy this?
Then it comes to you:
Trust you will be taken seriously.
Let flow your thoughts unfiltered,
your words resound uninterrupted.
Wear animal prints.
Check your chakra.
Shake your mudra maker.
Sing your sangha.

At last, emerging from the colors of their own nirvana,
few eyes open to see
another black woman
stop the clock, acknowledge
what is, and emerge ready to re-engage,
this time not playing the game.

From the Lighthouse
Dedicated to all who have dealt with adult onset mental illness

Here, amidst the circling light,
I don't need to see the sea to remember
the rocky waters we traversed. Back then,
on our journey for two
even keel was not an option.
Still, we rode the waves to sunset,
when a storm seduced us further from shore.

We tried to toe the line, had to,
then sat beneath the quiet eye
wet and laughing at our lucklessness.
We thought we were prepared, but
we had no way to be.

The waves came steady as a heart beating
until the quiet after
when they reached over
and pulled you in.

How the vessel grew
        big as dawn
to hold your absence
and carry me home.

I don't need to see the sea to remember
I miss you, still
being carried away
        on waves of madness.
May the water take you
        to where the wind could not.
And may you know my love
        even as I leave the lighthouse.

Coming Down

It was the year they toppled
the twin towers,
and our friend's doctor daughter
never rose from her birthing bed,
the year everybody said goodbye to somebody
leaving for lower price tagged living.
You came to me like a rain cloud
building over parched earth.   That year,
our first sprinkled kisses splashed, electric,
aroused rumbling echoes as
trepidation trickled a(muddy, murky)way.
We needed what the other offered—
your belly's moist touch reaching
for my packed soil yielding
to your slow grove dripping
into my wanton crevice aching.
Gravity guided your ripening into my embrace.
And somehow, I was uplifted
by your full weight
coming down on me.

Sidelined
Dedicated to blended families everywhere

She parents like she's coming in off the bench.
Been coached forever, but the real thing—well,
growth chart chalk marks don't tell
what to do, where to be like
coach's sideline sketching.
As a bench-born *you got this* echoes,
roused stock break fast
and, here she go,
up court, down court—sprints
to prove she can keep up with the starters,
always dribbling away.
Sees her way to the goal,
stretches, signals for a pass but
she's still too second string
to see her way home.
And when she expects a handoff,
they grow up, decide to do it solo—
a would-be assist lost
in the shadow of the single spotlight
again. She got picked, but can't roll with it.
Finally, she gets her groove
then comes a time out. But she goes back in, trusts
the timing, prays on position, and
makes a shot so sweet
it out shadows the final score.

Off court and on, she knows
she chose her jersey.
No matter how clean, it blends in,
makes them all a team. Now
she looks forward
to every season,
gets an endless high
just from playing the game

Switch Hitting

Ruth remembers
    orange dust airborne on spring breezes,
    dugouts speckled with sunflower seed shells,
       the snuff of little league.

That was the second year
    girls were allowed to play.
But Ruth didn't care, then,
    as nine freshly stained uniforms
    moved closer toward home.

Switch hitting couldn't be so hard.
Seemed ten times easier
    than her last dare.
In that batter box instant,
       she felt grown
   until, three pitches later
   when cheers died and
       Coach glared, then stared at his feet.

Ruth remembers
    the first year softball was played in the Olympics.
Through hospital gown, she rubbed small circles
on her mother's tender flesh
    more gently than she'd once knuckled
      her sweat-lined glove.

It now sits, somewhere,
       back in a closet,
   as antiseptic uniforms
      close in on her.
This time
      who has permission
      to grant, to deny?
Pondering, she feels eight again
      awkwardly switch hitting
  in the last inning
      of her mother's final season.

When I Arise

In the shower
my song can burst forth
for I feel safe
   where groomed by liquid phalanges.

I stop and breathe, while
enveloped in water,
enclosed in my tub,
safe in my bathroom,
deep in my apartment—
I'm in the womb of my living space.

I feel my body's temperature rise
   to meet that of the water's
   as I reach for my soap,
   my brush
   my implements of deconstruction
      are needed
      though I have already consented to
      washing my shit
      down the drain.

I need the water as it kneads me,
   loosening my tense head, shoulders, neck...

I come to consciousness
   grasping my showerhead microphone,
   it as wet with my spray as I with its.
And I realize I have forgotten
   the world outside my curtain

and so,
        relaxing my chest,
        expanding
        contracting my diaphragm,
        breathing as easy as a melody...
                "I can feel it
                moving,
                moving on the altar
                of my heart
                every now and then."

And when I arise glistening from the shower,
I am always surprised by the clean,
                bronze woman I see in the mirror.
She stands proud and naked before me.
Only she expected—demanded even
        the peace-filled eyes
        that return her bold gaze.

Additional Acknowledgements

For my first chapbook, *Sweating It Out*, I owe thanks to many, including:

- my family, given and chosen, for believing in me and my works year after year;
- the members of my feminist writing group—Akasha (Gloria) Hull, Celine-Marie Pascale, Helen Resneck-Sannes, Mercedes Santos, and Carol Whitehill—years ago in Santa Cruz, California, for their expert attention and endless encouragement;
- the entire team at Finishing Line Press who've made my manuscript shine;
- countless audience members who listened to me and let me know they heard; and,
- all those with whom I've played.

I extend a high-five to Virginia Woolf for her 1927 classic, *To the Lighthouse*, which inspired "From the Lighthouse."

Of the many who've supported my craft and provided me with opportunities to strengthen it, I can only thank a fraction in this space: Renee (Lynda) Brown (in memoriam), Cheryl Clarke, Connie Croker, Elizabeth Davenport, Rob Guillen, Kimberly Hughes, Jacquelyn Marie, Harry Meserv (in memoriam), Anne Nurse, Ekua Omosupe, Catherine (Cassie) Rubald, Amber Sumerall, Melinda Weil, Christopher David West, and Mardi Wormhoudt (in memoriam); my fellow Santa Cruz County Arts Commissioners; Ellen Bass and participants in one of her Writing Workshops; and, organizers and participants of the UCSC Women at Work Retreat and the In Celebration of the Muse annual events.

Here's a heartfelt, post-game hug to Akasha Hull who encouraged me to turn my first jock poem ("Switch Hitting") into a series.

Finally, I extend a sincere thanks to Mitchell Harrill-Wright, who tried to teach me how to play ("My Son's Avatar"). And, I so appreciate how Sandy Harrill engages (and, sometimes, bests) me in no end of play, serious and otherwise. I'm ever grateful for her loving and laughter.

Deborah Turner comes from a long line of tall woman. Coaches quickly spotted and recruited her for basketball, rowing, softball, and track, which help inform this collection of what she's come to call her *jock poetry*. She played the prior two in college (University of California, Berkeley) and remained in higher education long enough to earn her doctorate (University of Michigan; University of Washington). A librarian, educator, and researcher, she now writes full-time.

Her creative works convey a sense of redemption, hope, and the ability for all to do better—a sentiment that resonates in today's world that is frequently missing a sense of optimism. In *Sweating It Out*, she strives to show us another side of discovering and breaking rules of engagement whether in community, family, love, or sport. *Philadelphia Stories* and several collections, including *Philadelphia Says: Black Lives Have Always Mattered* and *Testimony*, feature her works.

Turner likes the dimension added to her creative works by reading them aloud to an audience and has done so in Arizona, California, Georgia, Michigan, New York, Pennsylvania, Washington, and—during her time as a Fulbright Fellow—Finland. Depending on the season, you may find her puddle jumping or catching leaves while biking or walking. Currently, she's working on a memoir based on her life in West Philadelphia; her first novel, *Harvesting Her Own Cranberries*; and, more poems.

To obtain a reading and discussion guide for *Sweating It Out* or to learn more about Turner and her works, please refer to www. deborahturner.online.

CPSIA information can be obtained
at www.ICGtesting.com
Printed in the USA
LVHW111305090321
680887LV00020B/2809